As They Taught Me...

Life Lessons Learned from

or

Influenced by Women in My Life

As They Taught Me...

Life Lessons Learned from

or

Influenced by Women in My Life

A'von McKenzie

ISBN: 978-0-9983676-8-2 (paperback)

Library of Congress Control Number:2019909088

Unless otherwise mentioned, Bible verses were retrieved from BibleGateway.com (public domain).

Skull and Crossbones image provided by Microsoft® Clip Art

Referenced articles found on Psychology Today (www.psychologytoday.com) written by C. Ross (2012) and Psych Central (www.psychcentral.com) E. Weinstein (2018)

With a Capital M Publishing Group, LLC

P.O. Box 52656

Durham, NC 27717

www.withacapitalm.com

withacapitalm@gmail.com

Special discounts are available on quantity purchases by corporations, associations, and others. For details, contact the publisher at the address above.

Dedication

I have to begin this book by first saying hello and welcome to the pages of my heart and mind. I came up with this idea while reading a magazine story and feeling proud of a mother for the sacrifices she was making for her daughter. Then I read a quick insert regarding hair care products and how another woman went natural so that her daughter would embrace her beauty (about a year ago I did the same). Not much later I had a title and a cover idea, and had sent the first of many series of group texts asking permission to use various friends' and family members' experiences as they relate to my personal inspirations and life lessons.

So, to all of the women in my life, around my life, written about and portrayed as characters... Thank you.

A special thank you to my husband and my children. Without them, I would never have the courage to put pen to paper. To my mother and grandmother and aunts, my foundation is strong because all of you are.

To you reading this book, thank you and may my love be felt in these pages and may you find at least one example you can apply to your life.

Preface

Let me begin by dispelling any thoughts you may have about me. I am no one special, yet I am as special and as magical as anyone who is to be admired throughout history and time. I have nothing, I came from a modest if not low-income neighborhood in Miami. I'm not talking the Miami of the music videos of today, *Love & Hip Hop*, or South Beach. I am southern by location and Caribbean by decent. I was born, raised and spent a good part of my life in Florida. I come from a family whose roots are strong in parts of the beautiful islands of the Bahamas. I was born and raised in an area known as Brownsville just on the other side of the more commonly known Liberty City. My neighborhood was comprised of working-class families living paycheck to paycheck: unrepresented people of America we all can relate to whether we ever acknowledge it or not. So again, nothing special. What does make me unique is the resilience I learned while growing up, because in order to be present-day me I had to have lived as I lived. That is not to say that I lived an especially risky life; it was filled with as many ups and downs as a young black woman in the world can have.

I was preyed upon and I was loved. I was ungrateful. I was allowed to believe from a very early age that my opinions actually mattered and that one day what I say and do would greatly influence those around me. I was disobedient and I was adored for my willingness to always give a helping hand. More than anything I have always been and will always be complex. It is within my complexity that I find my greatest joy and what brings me to want to share the anecdotal similarity I have come across while living life. Let me also say I do not come from with an extensive academic background, and I am not in any way trying to teach you anything at all, nor could I ever make suggestions about your lifestyle. I wanted to write this to boast of our similarities, especially when we often feel so alone. Though we may have differences in skin color, monetary holdings, or geographical locations, we have similarities: they lie in our ability to look outside of ourselves, embrace each other and the world, and work to make our impact and unique talents known. This is where I choose to begin.

I grew up around wonderful women and men who stressed and showed the importance of family, education, awareness, and faith. My grandparents were angels on earth for the time they were here, and they continue to be angels above guiding all my family and me.

My family shared many good times, and hopefully when my children grow up and become adults they will have as many good memories as I did. My most basic life lessons were about the importance of having clean surroundings: for example, bathe every night so that you don't bring the dirt of the day into your bed. How can you consider yourself clean in a dirty environment? Another lesson was that the key to truly being good looking is a controlled top and bottom (a.k.a., girdles and a good bra). They also showed me that it doesn't take money to have a good time. Every holiday was a time to celebrate with family and friends, and every Sunday was a time to thank the Most High Lord for every breath and morning and step you are able to take. (I'm sure others' gods and holy times gave them similar experiences.) More than anything, the women in my family taught me about strength and endurance.

My dad has nine brothers and sisters including a twin, which was not uncommon for the time he was born. What I have always liked about my family is that it was always blended. When my grandad claimed my grandmother as his own, he came into the relationship with four children who had just lost their mom, and my grandmother (who would happily claim that my grandad tempted her from her man) also had four kids. Add in the twins and there you have it folks, a family of twelve living in a three-bedroom home in South Florida. (My mom unfortunately was not as lucky and as well surrounded but we will discuss that in a little bit.) With those aunts, uncles, and grandparents, there has never been a time when I felt alone or unloved and cared for, but I have felt my shares of life's unfair cruelties and wished for something more. Of my dad's many brothers and sisters there was one who has always stood out to me, my Aunt G. She was the most like my grandmother in my eyes, and I adored her. I remember once letting it slip from my mouth that I wished my aunt was my mom instead of my mother, with the intent of hurting my mom's feelings. I guess in retrospect I was successful because, because when I awoke the next day (kidding, really just kidding, she never hit me that hard) I may have wished a little harder for different parentage, but I learned there was some things you just can't say. Aunt G is a little woman, she can't be any bigger than 5'4", but she absolutely commands a room when she enters it. She used to carry this huge jumble of keys and keychains, the amalgamation of places she had been and keys to various houses, a tangible representation of how many people relied upon and trusted her to take care of them both in person and by representation. There was this one key adornment in particular that was the equivalent of a deadly weapon if you had asked twelve-year-old me. It was a long-braided piece of material, like the friendship bracelets kids used to make out of colorful wire—but it had to be a least a foot long and at the end of the braiding the four strands, each knotted to control unraveling. It was a bit dingy and rough from being attached to her keys but never mind that, it was ever present. The significance of this keychain was that she used it as an unbiased weapon whenever someone was out of line, which was pretty often in a house that seemed always filled. I still smile when I think back on the spankings any of us could and would receive if we stepped out of line or had too much mouth for her taste. When I say any of us, I do mean all of my family. Children and parents alike were subject to catching the whip of that keychain if you couldn't move fast enough. She would ask for something to be done, and you had all of five minutes to do it before she would grab her keys and hit you with this cord. Funny how that is a good memory. When some people hear the word spank, they see it in a negative light, but I don't. Well, at least not always. Yes, as a child I received punishment spankings, and I won't dare claim that I saw all of them as necessary or welcome in the least. To be honest, some of my punishment sparked downright hatred inside of me but explaining that will be for another day. In this case her punishment was a show of love, equal expectations and the pecking order that happens within bigger families. The older siblings are usually charged with keeping the others in line. That's exactly what Aunt G did and she did it well.

My family believes in respect, tolerance, forgiveness, and joy…joy in family, joy in life, joy within yourself. Please, believe me, this whole book will not be all about my family, but you show me a person whose knowledge does not begin with family or lack thereof, and I'll give them a hug and tell them it'll be okay.

I adored my family, but as I grew older, I adopted a new one. This "family" represents the people I chose to allow into my life and influence my decisions, good, bad, or neutral. Not all of them lasted through the years but they all managed to teach me something. Sometimes these lessons hurt but each person helped me to build myself and discovery exactly what I am able to do. Every heartbreak helped me improve the strength of my heart, and every betrayal helped me build up my defenses. All my choices, interactions, and lack thereof are the makings of me, and I do love the me I see.

1

When I consider the most valued lessons I learned in life, the first to come to mind is about hygiene. Of course, we know all the obvious milestones of any person's life: we are born, we grow, we learn to eat, and we learn to desire things and we learn to recognize you have the ability to fulfil your own destiny. Well fin my home, what was equally important to at least one of my parents from the age of three to high school, was making sure I/we wore clean underwear. She obsessed about it, long after it made sense to. When I was younger, as long as my favorite cartoon character was on my underpants, I would wear it clean or dirty, it didn't matter. I just wanted to be Wonder Woman, or like my Cabbage Patch doll. Though I did what I was told, Mom had a hard time impressing the importance of hygiene on me. She would harp on about mundane stuff like putting the clean ones in my drawer, and how I wipe my butt. Who cares Ma!? As a child, I just didn't get why that was her pet peeve. As I got older, her insistence irritated me more; she would always say, "What if you get into an accident, do you want them to cut off your clothes and find you wearing dirty drawers?" As a budding teen, I found this to be peculiar, unnecessary, and just annoying.

It wasn't until I was about fifteen years old that I finally understood that not only was she being a nuisance about this because she loved me but also because it wasn't an option for her when she was a child. You see, my mother was not unlike most women growing up; she lacked the means and the guidance to make her life all that she wanted it to be. She was raised mostly by her the woman she chose to call grandmother, with no siblings. She had an absentee, drug-addicted mother not considering recovery. She never knew who her father was. My mother raised herself; she had to figure out daily where her next meal would come from and if she had a bed at night, and something as simple as clean laundry were not guaranteed, let alone having basic supplies that a young girl like my daughter would find an everyday necessity, such as wipes, soaps (bar or liquid), deodorant, and so on. The first time my mom opened up to me about her own hardships while growing, I felt like the worst child a parent could wind up with. My heart, as selfish as it often was, broke for her. I couldn't understand how anyone would allow their child to leave in such a neglected state. It was also my aha moment. I then understood and appreciated her concerns. No, she was not a raging, annoying, silly, petty woman; she was a child whom no one cared to check on. So the smallest things were of great importance to her, especially when raising her own family and her only daughter.

Only with understanding can we begin to empathize with those key individuals in our life. I got it now—you see Mom? I would tease and pull down a corner of my pants to do my version of show and tell, I match. The rewarding slight but definite smile that would grace her always-tired face was all the encouragement I needed to continue in my diligence of cleanliness. Perhaps it also developed my current obsession with pretty and frilly little things (little meaning the smallest piece of clothing I could wear but I am not a little girl *wink*), and I have an abundance of them. That smile was the beginning of my desire to purchase her such things as well. The first bra and panty combo I bought for my mom brought her to tears. Her reaction made it clear that I could ever love another person more than my mom and my own children. So, no big surprise to you that I find myself repeating a similar saying to my own daughter, who is a budding teenager herself.

Lesson 1

The Makings of:
What EveryBODY Has in Common

I can recall many occasions when things I had been told or taught by the women in my family came in handy. For example: when a girl begins her transition into womanhood, it's far from the beautiful and empowering process television would like you to believe. It's a bit disgusting—your body, hormones, voice, and growth all go haywire and you aren't in control of any of it. The physical changes to your body are random and sometime painful, and your voice loses all its baby cuteness and takes on depth and power it didn't possess before. They say your body changes, but in the mind of a child it feels like your body betrays you. Your body goes through so many changes, you never quite feel yourself, nothing about its growth is in your control no matter how may time you repeat the prayer for bigger boobs. Your limbs grow overnight—I mean you go to bed in one size and wake up looking like an extra in the movie *Big*. You start to feel things, I mean *feel things*; suddenly crossing and uncrossing your legs while wearing pants is a great idea. Your intimate parts, with all their new sensations, also carry an unfamiliar fragrance and if you are a tomboy like at least 50% of young girls are if you aren't mindful of these changes then that au natural fragrance is more akin to an odor, than the floral scent that media and pharmaceutical companies like to have you identify with.

There is a new desire to be seen as attractive or cute to the sex or sexes of your desire. Wait a minute, let me expound on that... One minute you and your friends don't care about anything other than getting outside and playing until you are forced to come in, and the next you want to be noticed. Not only noticed! You care what clothes you wear, and you also abuse colognes and perfumes like they were meant for you to bathe in. You start to resent your rate of growth in areas that were previously unnoticed, you notice how much your body changes and changes it shape. Depending on your influences you will notice that you may not look as you expected; you may be smaller or bigger than what you determine to be ideal. Chubby baby cheeks make way for actual cheekbones and defined bone structure, you may develop a fuller backside and wider hips or it might seem like your legs are the longest part of your anatomy. *Oh my goodness, what the heck is going on?* Suddenly tissue stuffing and striking a pose is essential to your health and wellbeing. Meanwhile, your parents suddenly are hearing sirens and warning bells going off and putting bars on the windows and doors.

There are three major changes a woman's body will experience, each marking a milestone in age and experience, Puberty, having a child or hearing the eternal clock chiming its reminder that it's now or never and that great day when Aunt Flow, the wicked visitor of the south, ceases to visit, otherwise known as menopause. When your body goes through the first of three major changes in its lifespan you believe that you are on the fast track to be the best thing since sliced bread. The only problem is learning how to control yourself. So allow me to suggest a few things, not as an expert on anything, but from the perspective of a woman who remembers these things all too well.

First let's confront BO (body odor); it happens to us all and doesn't ever stop being a problem until death do you part, so the sooner you get used to using the wide variety of deodorants available to you the better. Parents should really start their children using these products as soon as they hit a double-digit age. Sometimes even earlier. The key is to make it a part of their everyday routine. As babies become toddlers, who turn into walking, talking, entitled children with opinions and moods, the one thing I learned is initially having more responsibilities means you see them as capable, which in turn translates to being seen or of being responsible, you know it's the smile that comes with the praise you are such a big girl (or boy). If we parents are lucky, they idolize us from an early age and they crave to mimic any and every thing we do. So, allow your child to go through the getting-ready routine in the morning with you. Give them a child's equivalent to everything you use, as appropriate. Brush their teeth with kid-approved toothpaste and brush, give them a comb and brush, and maybe for deodorant they could use talcum powder, which has the same benefits and won't alter their body's balance. This will make things loads easier on both of you. Make the routine seem normal, and then when the body does change, you won't have to fight with them as much. Also, make bathing fun for babies and toddlers. More people ought to make it equally as fun as they grow past the age of five. Instead of bubbles for bubbles' sake, introduce body soap and oils. Give them new undergarments, appropriately sized of course, as a reward instead of a necessity. Reinforce the beauty of cleanliness and looking your best, always dressing as you wish to be viewed by the world, and I guarantee you're off to a great start in raising an awesome human being.

Train up a child in the way he should go, and when he is old, he will not depart from it. Proverbs 22:6, New King James Bible.

2

As I stated before, there are two versions of family you are likely to have: the one you are born into and the one you choose. My chosen family is made of the most important people in my life from around fourteen to today. Many of the friendships I made directly dictated the flow of my year; if I surrounded myself with good people then I was more likely to have a good year. But in my early teens that was the furthest thing from my mind.

From the making of your first friend to the last, one of the top concerns will always be whether you have fun when together. Depending on what you are exposed to, fun can mean many things. In my case fun was always about getting out from under my parents' ever-watchful eyes and letting loose. That way I learned about my own likes and dislikes.

Sometime around sixteen and a half, I believed I was ready for the world, that I was an adult who no longer needed my overbearing parents to tell me what to do. I have to laugh at that craziness. As they say—whoever *they* are—"If I only knew then what I know now"...geesh.

My first set of preferred family was colorful, to say the least. I chose to occupy my time with the second- or third-tier popular kids from my school. All of us knew everything—and nothing. It's a wonderful heady feeling to feel that nothing is better than what you know and have experienced thus far. Teenagers think they are invincible. My preferred family was comprised of like-aged girls and, surprisingly, not many boys at that time (we were all talk and spirit). I made many plans to hang out and party; school work and preparedness were at the bottom of our list. We had to hook up and stay on top of who's dating whom and what they wore while they were making up and breaking up. It was all very relevant to the directions our lives were heading—after all, we were going to be famous actors, musicians, and rappers, and of course I was going to have so many books published I couldn't keep up. (Ha, that's the biggest joke of them all, but I am still trying.) Together we were each other's everything After all, our parents didn't know us. Shoot, they never even knew where we were.

We were as thick as thieves. Sometimes we were thieves. You did things because you could get away with it, and if now and then you actually got in trouble for your actions, even then it was still a small price to pay to hang with your friends. Outside of that first real boyfriend or girlfriend, your friends are your world, but there comes a time when every friendship is tested, and it is in those times when you truly start to develop your character. Accusations of cheating, lying, boy- or girlfriend stealing, sexual looseness, and style have torn many friends apart. I lost many friends while developing my character, sometimes because they didn't fit into that first lesson (hygiene) or how they carried themselves was wrong; if I couldn't stand beside you without being embarrassed or feeling like you reflected poorly on me, then we couldn't be friends. In hindsight this made me the bad friend, and they were better for not having me around, but in the moment leaving them was funny.

I took it even further: as my friend, it was required that I could tell you anything and if need be you would harbor me on any number of my efforts to run away, because run away I did. I ran as often and as far as I could, once I hit the golden age of sixteen. I thought my parents didn't know me, didn't love me, and didn't understand me. They were keeping me away from enjoying the version of life my friends were living, and in my immature mind that was downright criminal. So, if a person was willing to give me a safe place to sleep and something to wear, then they were considered a friend, and in return for that friendship, I had their back through thick in thin; I would fight for them, lie for them, and harbor them if ever I could. Nothing would end my friendships except that person purposefully becoming toxic and harmful. That didn't mean that my friends and I didn't suffer through the aforementioned ailments of most friendships (cheating, lying, etc.). It just meant that we could argue or not speak, but at the end of the day if they held up your end of the bargain, so did I. Every secret, every conversation, every indiscretion was locked away in the deepest vault within me in exchange for that sacred friendship. To this day my loyalty remains the same.

Lesson 2

What You Teach, They Will Sow and Spread

My mother was a hard nut to crack on the outside—and the inside too. She didn't take any sh*t...ever! She loved fiercely and made no excuses for her actions or words. I absolutely hated and loved her for that. She could be lifelong friends with someone (many of these friends I called aunties, but had no relation), but if she perceived them as having broken a friendship rule, she cut them off. No questions asked and no reasons guaranteed. Although I can't say that I agree with how quickly and completely she cuts off those connections with people, I have always admired her standing her ground and holding onto her principles of friendships. So, when it comes to making friends and separating them into categories of life-long, momentary, associate, and "yeah, I know them," I use the same decisive methods as I saw my mother do growing up.

There were many times when I needed to be told I was screwing up both in and out of school. There were times when I let my heart lead me right into trouble on the streets, breaking rules my parents set for me. There were times when friends didn't like the influence of other friends had on me and depending on the category or their concerns, if I found them valid at the time, my actions changed, or I fell further and further away from my true path. My friends saved my life on many occasions. Whether a person knows it or not, they want like-minded people in their corner, walking the path together to that promised level of riches waiting to be found. Without a solid foundation and example from the first friends you ever had, your family, especially your cousins; you'll never create a world that best represents you.

This, of course, comes into play when you have your first teenage outings. If your friends don't look "right" when they come and knock on your door, you knew there was no way your parent was going to let you go any further than the porch, if that. So, your choice is either to plan to deceive or plan to stay at home, trouble chooses trouble. That is not to imply at all that people can't change; it is just more likely that the process will take longer if everyone involved is following the wrong leader.

For example: Friend A and I were discussing plans to skip school and hook up with our boyfriends, something we had been doing for a few weeks. At this point I was eager to agree because I was no longer afraid of getting caught. My grades were suffering, but as long as I didn't fall below a C– I could skirt past my parents. They were too busy with work to care anyway, and my other friends had stopped asking me why or trying to stop me as long as I wasn't gone the whole day. One or two classes missed was fine! At least that was my rationale.

Needless to say, I was in more trouble after a while than I could ever imagine and those spankings that created hatred within me were becoming the norm. I was angry a lot, and I thought that everyone sucked (these are the rambling of a teen, so don't judge me, OK). I was a terror to be around for a short period of time I'm sure, but as long as my friends and I had each other backs nothing else mattered... Until I thought I was pregnant for the first time.

My world came crashing down around me. All I could do was panic, hyperventilate, and pray. Of course, my ace boon coon was nowhere to be found when I wanted to tell her. When I finally did speak to her, she was all, "Oh for real? Damn girl whatcha gon' do?" I thought this chick had sprouted horns and was completely unrecognizable, but that couldn't be true, right? We were thick as thieves! I assumed she was either possibly pregnant too or she had a plan to help a sister out. Nope, all she had was no time for me; I was slowing down her efforts to meet her boo. In my biggest time of need, my "friend" was nowhere to be found. So, I dragged my way back into the good graces of my other friend, previously thought of as nagging. Not only did they dry my tears without ever murmuring, "I told you so" (at least loud enough for me to hear), but they held my hand and talked me back into the right side of wrong. Thank goodness I was not actually pregnant at the tender age of seventeen and, more importantly, I never let my parents or grandparents know anything was ever amiss.

What I learned was, people are all around you, and anyone can call themselves your friend, but when things really get hard and your butt is truly on the line, only a real friend will be still standing there, judgment in one hand, but offering the other to you to hold, willing to lend you a sympathetic ear and putting off the I-told-you-so look until a later time when they can smack your head. If you are as lucky as I have been, you will have one or two or five of those people in your life. They will be with you through the thick and the thin of all life throws your way. They will remember every embarrassing moment and every time your heart was broken. They hold your secrets and celebrate your successes. So, take my advice: choose wisely. Choose the type of people whom you could grow old with, because friendship is a lot like marriage, if you're lucky. And choose wisely. They will be with you until death you do part.

3

One of my favorite phrases of my adult life is, "That's not appropriate." I like this one because it applies to so many things and situations in today's world. When I think back to my developing years, there were so many inappropriate experiences. Kids' ability to blend into the background makes for many an inappropriate conversation overheard. You get to hear about who is in rehab, who fell off the wagon, and who slept with whom. This is how I found out exactly how rampant drugs were in both sides of my family, as several of my family members struggled with addiction. Of course, overhearing these things didn't make them any more understandable to me. But it did explain why my uncle would move in and out of my grandparent's house and why each time he left something else was missing. Or why my cousin went away for years at a time and each time he came back he looked beefy. I'm sure those would have been deemed inappropriate conversation for a young girl to hear. Inappropriate conversations for children are any that would expand their awareness of life before their due time. Conversations about sex or sexual activity even when had in jest if not explained properly or without context could easily give a child a false impression of what is acceptable. Appropriateness is however subjective; it is in the eye of the holder of said information and for them to discern whether that information is necessarily shared in mixed company. Basically, it tickles me to say, "That's not appropriate," because it's a sweet way of saying, "Mind your business and stay out of mine."

Puberty seems like it should be an innocuous stage of life when you think that all the world's citizens have to go through it, yet it also brings about its own share of inappropriate settings, especially for a young girl whose body is developing a more mature shape. The people around her tend to notice long before she does and become very handsy. I really think that the word puberty should always appear in red and with a skull and crossbones symbol next to it whenever written in text! ☠ Parents, if you're lucky, the full extent of it will blow by in a breeze, and the worst experience will be when your child begins dating. Having and housing a dating teen is not easy, not at all; my mother would be the first to attest to that.

Alongside puberty comes the need to have "The Talk," from a non-abstract point of view. Every parent should be very clear with their child not only as to what's allowed and what is considered appropriate touching, whether from friends or from a family member, but also that is allowed to have the expectation of privacy and boundaries. Meaning it is no longer and perhaps it never was right to sit on your uncles' lap.

Imagine this if you will: from birth you have looked into the eyes of your child, niece, nephew, or grandchild and loved them with an immensity you never knew possible. This sweet little person would shower you with more kisses and hugs than you could ask for. They looked to you for guidance and understanding; you vowed to protect them and love them and teach them everything you know. You learned to view the world through their eyes and your faith in humanity was renewed, all because they exist. Imagine that person one day standing in front of you with hands on hips, rolling their eyes and talking back. I assure you that if there is a Twilight Zone you have been escorted into it and have front row seat to the show. Where did your sweet, innocent little kid go and who is this alien standing in front of you? You will wonder over and over again what went wrong. When did you step left when you obviously should have gone right? Who did you harm in your past life that this person you have vowed to rear into a respectable adult turn into a spitfire tween or teen who has outings planned, clothing that's two sizes too small, the shape of someone twice their actual age, and the mouth of a burgeoning sailor? What exactly are you supposed to do as the parent of said child? You can't lock them up and throw away the key. You can't discipline them beyond taking away electronics or (oh so effective) grounding them. These days spankings are corporal punishment in the eyes of public opinion. You can't very well jump in that time machine and fast forward to their college graduation so here's my advice...

Lesson 3

Appropriate Behavior For An Inappropriate Child

Although several years have passed since early childhood, the rules are still the same. It is your job as a parent (no matter how you came across the title; whether birth, step-, or godparent) to set and enforce rules and appropriate disciplines for your child. Boundaries are a child's best friend; they just don't know it. Without rules and consequences, you can expect for puberty to be twice as hard and seem twice as long. Also, you should know children mimic the behaviors they see and hear as they grow and develop. Now I'll be the first to admit that having children does damper the fun of being an adult. Hence the decision to procreate should be done when you're ready. But being realistic, how many people today can claim that they planned their pregnancy and were fully prepared? All that said, if you raise your child in a toxic, overstimulated environment then hey, you reap what you sow (as I said in lesson 1). An article by Dr. Carolyn C. Ross, MD, in 2012 argued that children exposed to sexually explicit behavior at an early age or are victim to sexual abuse early in life are twice as likely to become promiscuous early in life and sometime use sex or their sexuality as an answer or a way to get things they want. In a 2018 study posted in Pyschcentral.com, Edie Weinstein further explored the impact of early exposure of sexual related actions, activities and pornography have resulted in both and good and bad feelings on the then-adolescent. Feelings ranging from embarrassment to disgust between those exposed at an age as early as thirteen. Of course, this does not hold true for every child or every scenario, and there are those children who exhibit the exact opposite behavior. They are very introverted and closed off, they shy away from human contact and become clingy with those people they trust and consider safe. The common denominator will still be boundaries and expectations. You have a right to monitor the actions and behavior of your child; you have a responsibility to know what they do and whom they hang out with. You also have to know as much as you can about the people your child spends time with when they begin to exhibit their sexual awakening.

Three things are true in life: 1. If you turn a blind eye to things, you will be blindsided. 2. Children don't need a parental friend; they need a parent. 3. Inappropriate behavior at any age if not corrected will only get worse.

Kids testing the waters, a.k.a. pushing their boundaries, is normal, and all I can offer you as a parent is a wing and a prayer. Patience and support are key to surviving this phase in their life, but I promise you'll make it out of this okay. If all you have is love, then look around you for everything else you need to make it to the next stage in their ever-changing life.

4

So, we made it through all the rough stuff right, and there looks like there might be a light at the end of the tunnel. Whew, there is a bottle of wine that has been chilling since cat was a kitten (as my friend says). You can practically taste the fermentation of the grapes, and after giving up the majority of your social life when this thing called parenthood began, you can't wait to relive the good ole days of spring breaks gone by. Just as you settle down in your favorite chair and begin circling one-bedroom loft-style apartments and gauging that against what the market will look like in ten short years, the popular phrase "when an irresistible force, meets an immovable object" comes to life. What I am talking about is the aftermath of that bad word, puberty. One day not so far after the start of puberty your baby will wake up and have boobs, hair where there previously was none, and a sense of their own changes that will lead to locked doors, requests for privacy, and wanting more attention from peers—and make no mistake, *it will be sexual.* Everything is really topsy-turvy, pigs are indeed flying, and you really can't believe the changes that mount every day and night. They get taller, fuller, and sassier, and their choice in clothing changes; if you are lucky enough to have a girl (as I do), you have to buy bras and panties just because they think it's pretty.

You can't shop without them anymore because you don't "get" them and their style.

There is something else happening that is even more crucial, something unseen: the awareness that they are different. Different from childhood playmates and current classmates. When I say different it applies to a wide spectrum of things; there is a difference in skin color, hair length and type, eye color, religion, and more. Your child understands and reacts to these facts of life. You undoubtedly hope that they will remain stable and know that their individual differences are what makes them desirable and beautiful.

However, what is more likely to happen is that on top of them being keenly aware of the differences of those around them, they will also be aware of the ever-changing, very superficial, twice-as-critical world of social and celebrity media. All of which makes your compliments—whether seldom or daily—saying "you're beautiful, you're wonderful, you're talented, you're smart, yadda, yadda, yadda," that much more meaningless. If you're like me you can't even keep up with the most current rapper and what he really means when he says, "I'm so awesome out here like a possum." With the surplus of songs about booties, drugs, hustling, and bein' 'bout dat life (please forgive me), what can a parent do to help and manage successfully their child's self-esteem?

Lesson 4

They Are Not What They Hear, See, or Show

Providing your child with positive role models and intellectual stimuli used to be much easier. That's when the world was full of two-parent homes, grandparents who were appropriately aged, and resources that did not cost you a mortgage payment. In my case, as previously stated in chapter 1, I had aunts and uncles and cousin who all held me accountable for being as beautiful and wonderful a person as they told me I was every day. These days the family structure has changed quite a bit: the mom and dad are super busy trying to provide for said young adult, so they often feel accomplished just in their ability to keep the fridge stocked with whatever today's healthy initiative is and a requested junk food item or two. Aunts and uncles are nothing more than another set of parents, trying to duplicate the rules and schedule originally dictated in your home as to not look like the slacker in the family who aided and abetted in your corruption through spoiling practices and indulgences of whimsy; both praying that the ward in question doesn't kill, assault, or impregnate anyone before they turn eighteen, thus becominging the sole person to (legally) blame for their actions. Grandparents are a lot younger these days, so them being able to impart wisdom is an increasingly unlikely scenario. Of course, this is not true in every scenario but enough that it's worth mentioning.

So, allow me to play the part of an aunt or person you turn to when you need some help or guidance. First, if you are following my general theme here then you already know that this process would be a heck of a lot easier if you started it years ago, somewhere around birth or maybe even conception (if you're a person who feeds into the concept that the baby can hear you in the womb). You are and should always be your child's first source of positive reinforcement and encouragement. Listen to their concerns about their body image and try not to dismiss them as nonsense, because their concerns come from today's headlines. Don't compromise your standards and allow them to dress and act older than they are or act in a manner that would garner them unsavory attention, but maybe allow them to explore varying hairstyle, clothing, and makeup at home with you and a close friend as the judge. Kind of like an adult version of playing dress-up, allow them the space to explore and create their personal styles without ridicule and reprimand. This way they won't feel the need to hide or subdue their desire to be different, while still giving you the heads-up on their inner thoughts. Reinforce the importance of their diet and exercise in relation to body image and have fun with the tools of today: hair clip-ins of varying lengths and colors that "everyone else is wearing," makeup of appropriate age and setting (lip gloss and complexion-appropriate eye-shadow), and allow their exploration of social media websites with restriction on participation and access. Monitor their activities and outings without stifling them. Allow them to flourish and become the person you ultimately raised them to be, but please remember at the end of the day, this is your child. You are in control of their actions simply because without you they don't have the resources, the ability, or the financial stability to do the things that interest them. It goes without saying that you don't ever want them to turn to someone else for their wish list. So, try as hard as you can to not turn them away, recognize the pressure that your child feels in their need to conform and to be a part of their intended circle of friends.

You are the mirror and the definition of beauty and stability. All things begin and end with your acceptance of all their quirks and antics and behavioral changes. Be the model you want them to emulate. That does not mean you need to seem perfect or strive for perfection—quite the contrary. Show them your faults and your accomplishments, show them your efforts and your insecurities, show them the complexities of life, and I can assure you that you will be the best role model they could ever wish for. You will be showing them that nothing is life is easy, especially when it comes to an understanding yourself. You are an ever-changing thing, and the hope is that you never stop learning how to improve yourself both on the inside as well as the outer image most people see. Also, show them that reinvention is the best fun a person can have in a lifetime, and the coolest part about it is you are able to do it an infinite amount of times... The only thing that is hard to change is bad reputation. So always be your best self, no matter what differences you have.

Interlude

I intend to share all the perspectives I have been given and gifted for the purposes of sharing knowledge with anyone who has seen or gone through the trials and joy of raising children. After years of living and commiserating with friends and family about the trials of trying to raise children as we were raised in a time where technology rules our world, I figured that my memories and my skills make me uniquely qualified to give my unwarranted opinion to the masses. Because that is what we have come to, right, so why not throw my hat in the proverbial ring of "my opinions matter so much I need to broadcast it to the public foray"—see daughter, I do know about *Keeping Up with the Kardashians*—that and I just like writing books. So there you have it.

I cherish every part of growing up and being blessed with children, but I do so aware of the struggles I went through. I had a troubled yet wonderful upbringing, and because I was raised among what I consider to be an Island American household, my experiences are slightly different from what used to be the masses, as the world becomes increasingly diverse maybe not so unique anymore. I was what I now know as working middle class; we were not poor, nor rich. I for the most of my upbringing had a two-parent household with aunts and uncles who allowed me to dream without focus. Dreaming, unbeknownst to me at the time, is an important part of being a kid—it allows you to envision yourself in a plethora of potential job fields, and that process of examining your future potential makes you more likely to pursue a higher education in efforts to achieve those dreams. However, I also grew up with people who had a singular focus of keeping on the right side of up; their dreams only allowed them to get as far as Friday night, when they could drink and find a semblance of merriment for as long as the Old English or MD 20/20 would allow their minds to slip. Being surrounded by others who did not dream of anything more them making it to their next paychecks left me feeling foolish for imagining myself not only living life but enjoying the life I lived. I was expected to work hard, eventually live home and hopefully not have more than one kid before doing so. More just wasn't something to strive for. As I grew older I realized that to dream is the right of all people born but to achieve the dreams was only the right of the driven and educated. Thus I found myself in a paradox, because I did not choose the path of education. This was not for lack of desire to learn but because I wasted chances with misdirection and bad choices. Growing up I did believe that achieving a higher education was the only way to ensure stability, financial and familial success, and that success in turn would grant my happiness. It took years of my life to release that notion and accept that not everyone who applies themselves and trudges forward towards the desired initials behind their name (e.g., MSW, PhD, LPN, etc.) is successful. Quite the contrary in my opinion; only those who choose happiness and make their paths regardless of status are truly successful in life. In fewer words, I am saying that a person who enjoys planting can either be a horticulturist or a gardener, solely based on the depth and perspective of their job. Same goes for most positions, the beautiful thing about life is the joy lies in how you the individual chose to live it. I truly believe there is pride found in the work of being housewife or -husband, just as there is joy in being a partner in a major law firm. The choices you make in life, where you end, no matter how late the start is what you will reflect upon later in life and hopefully you enjoyed the path you chose to take. Above all else choose joy, and work hard to achieve it.

Onward and upward we go.

5

Another commonality we have in life are the laws that govern our existence. We are born, and from that day ever forward we are marching on to our final breath. While we grow through the many stages of life one of the more poignant parts of said life is the awareness of our bodies' ability to give us pleasure.

One day not unlike any other, while trying to squeeze another five minutes into an already-late start, my stretch, moan, and groan felt different. They caused a jolt as I extended my legs to their greatest length. Just that squeezing of my legs together was my welcoming to the pleasure of my own body. Never had a stretch or rolling around in my childhood bed felt better. I had been woefully unaware that all it would take to turn my world upside down was a little friction and a slight bit of pressure at the apex of my thighs. Boys are expected to experience wet dreams early in life and whether there is ever a conversation had about it or not, it is such a known fact that around the age of twelve or thirteen that a parent will never want to touch anything in their son's room again without gloves, and Vaseline doesn't stand a chance.

Even the most pious of people will have to reconcile their sexuality and desire. Some may choose to turn their energy into outward devotion, others choose to use that energy to focus on doing good deeds and seemingly wholesome work all in an effort to redirect the sexual desires. The reason I say seemingly is because wholesomeness is in the eye of the doer, a person interpretation of a good deed may seem like a waste of time to another, what matters most is the effort and energy placed into the task in an effort to not expound that energy sexually. Most, however, go through these stages using exploration and indulgence to teach themselves about their likes and dislikes. This time should be seen as just as sacred and formative as any lesson you could learn in school. As an adult I realize the importance of knowing one's own peaks and valleys. The expectation that another person will magically know how to please you is absurd, just as it is not a good idea for a person to learn about sexual gratification through porn. Anything I could write won't help you figure it out either, but I would like to share my own experience, and hopefully, this will help at least one person make a better decision.

Love is disguised as sex. I thought about rewording that to say sex is disguised as love, but that's not exactly true. Every man, woman, and child wants to be loved by someone or something. Our interpretation of what love looks like is often disguised by sex because to be touched in a tender manner feels wonderful. Hence, why there are so many varying ways to discover your sexual self.

Now I know sex has become a commonplace word, but there was a time it was sinful and naughty to reference sex so casually. It comes with the connotation of lust, evil, unhealthiness, and lack of self-respect. Let me tell you about my experience and the turmoil of learning the good and bad of this natural stage of life.

At a very early age, I was awakened by the urges to touch myself. Never having even known that my lower half was to be used for anything other than going to the bathroom, sitting, running, and walking, this came as such a shock. Of course, I didn't understand it; one day I could sleep peacefully and have dreams of toys, dolls, and multicolored horses and bears. Seemingly overnight my day and night dreams were thoughts of being touched, caressed, desired, and loved. No one preps a girl for that accidental graze of her clitoris. There were a lot of feelings that surrounded that experience and as much as I felt comfortable talking to my mom about things, I didn't dare to bring this up. It was made worst during the day because being the churchgoing girl I was; I just knew I couldn't tell anyone about this. I couldn't ask my mother or friends if they had the same experiences and what did they do to solve it. Oh, and believe me, that's exactly what I wanted to do. I wanted to solve this mystery and make it go away. I didn't like this insistent throbbing that would not allow my soul to be still and innocent. I couldn't even understand what triggered it, what I did to make it start. I thought I must have done something wrong—maybe I had like-liked one too many boys. I felt guilt and shame. I wished it away and tried to ignore the building need. The desire to explore myself was never-ending, but it had to be bad, because no one ever talks about a girl pleasuring herself, right?

It didn't take long for me to shed my innocence and for me to see the world in a new light. I noticed the differences between girls and boys. I discovered the strength (even at early teen years) of men and the subtle beauty and wonderment of women.

I notice smells and the colors of heat that rises when a person is feeling desired. Oh, what a wonderland...but what should I do?

One day my friend from down the street came over to play, something routine and that I looked forward to. After all, growing up I only had until the streetlights came on to play outside with friends, and that time was already lessened because I had to waste what seemed like forever in school. On this day my friend wanted to play "House"; I would be the mom, and she would be the dad. Playing house is a lot like paying tea party except that at a certain age understanding and awareness plays a part in what you do. So, when our tea party turned into her version of play imitating life, I didn't know I was doing anything wrong. We lay next to each other pretending to go to sleep like mommies and daddies do and she touched me, not so much sexually. Still, to be touched in an intimate manner, even innocently, oh you wouldn't believe the colors I saw. Red, gold, purple fireworks. All I wanted was for her to do more, to be closer—to either stop or maybe create more of the same. She kissed me, and I looked at her...trying to find love. I didn't process any of this against right and wrong, because it just was us playing a game and me not wanting to stop. After all, hadn't we always played together, and hadn't I never broken any rules. So this must be okay, right?

The way my mother came into my room and broke us apart and loudly told my friend to go home, I'm guessing she didn't feel the same way. What the events of that day showed me was how much I didn't understand. I was a little girl, and I knew nothing other than I wanted to be with my friends because your friends always made you feel good. Remember...friends are the family you get to choose. The only problem I had was how I was going to see the fireworks again. Especially now because for some unknown reason I was grounded (my lips are pursed just remembering that). Grounded because I was playing? That didn't make any sense. I did not understand anything at this stage, but nothing was going to stop me from finding out all that I could. (Side note: Parents, sometimes your desire to protect takes away from the trust and communication you so desperately desire from your offspring.)

So, it was after that pivotal day that I yearned for sexual comfort disguised as love. Before all things were equal, one plus one, right, like I reconciled the affection of my parents hugging and kissing me as them showing me love, so naturally when my friend played with me, she must have been doing the same. (Do you see where I'm going with this?)

Lesson 5

We Are All Vulnerable, Impressionable, And Looking for Love

Here are a few facts:

1. Men, women, and children can all be victims of some type of sexual assault.

2. Sexual development begins with sexual awareness, and that awareness begins as early as the age of two.

3. If you don't inform or teach your child about their bodies and the changes it will go through, they will look for that information somewhere else. Oftentimes children learn through experience (as they did when learning to talk, walk, and eat).

4. The easiest way to understand something is to explore yourself and what is at your disposal.

5. If you make a child feel that something is wrong, they are four times more likely to hide that part of themselves from you, the person judging their action.

Everyone that wants to know now knows that many children are victim to sexual molestation or rape. Many women are taught that they encourage this attention because they are too flirty or dress proactively. People whom you could consider to be trusted or family are often the first persons to cause this infraction and many times these stories are untold or not believed. So oftentimes the child harbors a feeling of guilt and being unclean and unwanted. I am stating all this because I started off this chapter by saying that all people want to know and experience love and they choose many different ways in which to achieve it. The bottom line still remains that every person goes in search of it.

So here is my advice to you, a lot like the advice I've given already: Talk to your child. Be aware of them. Establish a truly open communicative relationship with them, even if what they have to say is difficult to hear.

I can almost guarantee that when their sexual awakening happens, it will be difficult to hear. You are their first teacher, so teach them with the numerous resources at your disposal. Don't neglect the difficult conversations because they make you feel uncomfortable. Violations are so much more complex than saying you should protect your private areas. (Thanks Ma for that.) Tell them *why* they need to be protected. Tell them about diseases and sex and their relation. Let them know that they will at some point experience an unfamiliar feeling and explain to them why. Never make them feel afraid to ask questions, even if you don't always have an answer. It is better to show your faults and them to close them out because you don't know. Of course, I have only touched the surface of this topic, I am only giving you a starting point for all the basis of raising a person. Hence the title of this book, *As They Taught Me*; "as" implies the beginning or the start of, not the end. It implies an ongoing process. So that's what I am giving to you: a beginning of a process.

6

What are we, if not what beauty was intended to be

We are the guardians and the guides

We are Persephone, empowered from birth and created to bring balance to all

We see the hidden talents, the brightness inside of thee

Who are they to judge the very essence that brought their existence to birth

We are the cornerstone and the damnation

We are the truth and the lie

We are the light buried deep in the muddy waters yet reflecting sunshine

We are not a tool to be used and discarded, we are the very empire that you seek

Who are we if not the bottom basic neuron that excites your mind and makes all men weak

What we do and what we know can bring any nation to kiss our toes

What we bear is the beginning and the end, we are the fruit and the curse

What we carry is...well, everything

Whom do you know better than we

We are Woman

Wonder and mystique

So, as we all transition in womanhood one thing is clear: we all have no idea what being a "woman" actually means. Sure, yes, we have the body parts, and Lord knows we get the full range of emotions to contend with, but what does it really mean? At my current age of forty, I still don't think I have a full understanding of what it means. I am a mother, which to some degree makes me a nurturer; I am a sister, which makes me protective; I am a daughter, which makes me responsible and caregiver. But do these constitute womanhood?

Well, let me tell you what I know, the definition of womanhood does not cover it at all. If most women are anything like me and other women I know, there is a part of them that always feels like a little girl. When you fall in love for the first or fortieth time, you feel just like a little girl. When your parent looks at you both in good and bad times, you feel like a little girl. When you and your friends get together and have a girls' night out, you feel 200% like a giggly teenage girl. Does that mean the only time you feel like a woman is when you are being a "grown-up" and doing the grown-up thing—being responsible and paying bills, going through life's changes, and feeling your heart ache? If those are the only times I can call myself a woman, then I renounce that title and create a new one: I am a grown-ass girl. Hmm, I like the sound of that; it sounds more encompassing and yet still fun. So, if anyone else feels like I feel, feel free to take on the title.

Lesson 6

Learning to Love Yourself and Keeping It Up

So as mentioned a time or two previously, my chapters and stories are mostly based on lessons learned throughout my life. This one, in particular, was more amusing to me than most, because it has a more recent understanding of an old principle.

I was a late bloomer, I didn't get a chance to explore furthering my education until my children were practically young adults themselves. (I had to be mature earlier than most people since I chose to have a family at nineteen.) Once given the opportunity I relished everything about it—I enjoyed every class and every friendship made, but specifically I appreciated my journey because it brought great prespective and understanding to each class I took. I was reminded while my class hosted a guest speaker about the process of finding ways to love yourself. She spoke in a laissez-faire manner about how growing up she was not taught that she should love herself, let alone how. This resonated with me deeply, it made me grateful to have the family that I have. My grandmother, mother, and aunts told me often that I was worthy of a better life and that I was beautiful and should be respected. For that I am grateful, but after my few years of life it is apparent to me that learning to love oneself isn't usually taught to young girls or young boys for that matter. Parents don't invest in their children as they used to; people invest in the economy, in the misery of others, and in material things or the assets that can be purchased to enhance themselves. There was a time when parent's greatest efforts were in the encouraging children as a whole to follow their dreams, develop their talents and build up their perspectives of self and their possibilities. When the focus is placed on how you look versus how a person feels about themselves, what is actually happening is you place value on the person as a commodity. At which point is there really any surprise why we have so many young men and women out in the world doing anything to "enhance" themselves. Yes, we love them, yes, we provide for them, and yes if lucky enough we pave a path for them after struggling ourselves to make a better life, but we don't often take the time to teach our children to love themselves. We place restrictions and expectations on our children and we fail to see what the pressures of those ideals do to them. Our children are born to love and adore us. It is their nature to want to be favorable, loved, and seen for their every effort, and if you are a standard parent, you are proud of them, you relish sharing their triumphs and joys, and you are trying ot make sure their next day is better than their last, but you are too busy to truly dote on them. So, what do you do? How do you break a cycle that is more damaging to them, our future adults? I'll come back to this a little later on.

7

You present yourself to me, you stand before me smiling and pass along a sheet of paper. This paper is meant to represent you and all that you know. Little do you know the paper is a mere accessory to all that I see before me. You are the package; you are the prize to be procured (not purchased!), then handled and developed into something that works toward my needs and your advancement. Though the image you present is well put together, it is what happens. next, that dictates whether we shall continue down this road together or if I shall send you on your way, although with the blessing of continued success and security. The next two minutes will tell me all that I need to know because through the years I have learned that all that glitters aren't gold. So I ask you to speak, to tell me a little more about yourself. It's with that first phrase that I am certain of two things: your intellect and your capacity for language and conversation.

That's right people, this chapter is all about the presentation of *you*. Have you ever wondered how you are perceived beyond your looks, or whether a person can get past your past? It has been said for years that you can't take back a first impression. What if when you first met a person, it wasn't in a favorable light—how do you correct that impression of you if ever you should meet again? People spend a lot of money trying to perfect they the way they look or the way they are perceived by the masses—and for a good reason! No person wants to be seen as less than or undesirable right. Here's the thing: there is something as caring too much about your appearance, especially when after you have presented yourself, the person you are is nowhere to be found. Have you ever searched YouTube for a makeup tutorial and found that people put on so much makeup you can barely tell their true ethnicity or facial features? Add in clothes and weaves and the person you appear to be is nothing like the person you truly are, and that is what you are presenting as your best self.

How then can you say that you put yourself forth? When you hide so much of yourself that also says a lot about the person you are. Yes, you may look beautiful, but honestly, a person can see your insecurity and vanity, and they may think that you can't possibly be taken seriously for an opportunity that would lessen your exposure. Because all that effort into making yourself up is because you aim to be seen, right? Of course, the opposite could be argued as well, it could be pointed out that your attention to detail and in your appearance is a sign of caring and pride. That's the dilemma when presenting yourself: the difference between what you think you are presenting and what they will see. Are you portraying confidence or cowardice? Do you value your outside strengths more than your skills? Do you think you are good enough and, if so, then what are you afraid of the world seeing?

Lesson 7

Beauty Is Better When It's More Than Skin Deep

Okay, so I don't know if I mentioned this or not, but one of my favorite movies is *Eat Pray Love* (Elizabeth Gilbert if you ever read this, find me...please). I love the opening of the movie when Julia Roberts is narrating about the women in the detention camp and her friend being anxious about what she would say to them, when all they want to talk about was love and their relationships. Well, I had a friend who would do something very similar: while making herself up, she would sit in front of her mirror discussing all the people who *might* see her and how she needs to look better than good in order to "catch her a good man." Meanwhile, I was and am the queen of comfort—if I can fit it, and it feels good, then I wear it. If it happens to accentuates my curves then it's a win-win. That, with a touch of gloss and eyeshadow, is the me you get.

So my friend and I were polar opposites when we stepped out the door, and I was always fine with that. If she wanted to be seen, then I would gladly allow her to take up all the space there was to give to achieve her goals. It never occurred to me that in doing so I could be sending a message that I thought I wasn't good enough to be seen first, or that I lacked confidence. Some people would interpret my occupation behind the scenes that way, just as much as some would see her thrusting herself forward as aggression and over-eagerness.

It took me several years and the feedback of good friends for me to realize that neither was preferable in life. Standing tall and demand to be counted for your values, your abilities, and your talents isn't a detriment to your perception. It won't appear to the outside world like anything other than you exuding confidence and a willingness to be present. If a person wins an achievement solely based on looks, then that is all they may ever be seen for, and once the looks fade, what will they have left? In the same breath, no one looks at the sheepish bookworm and says outright they are beautiful; not because they aren't, but because how would you ever know if their head is always down or they are standing in the back of the room holding up a wall?

8

Ever have that moment during an interview where you are trying to impress someone with your mental prowess as much as your individual strengths and skills? The type of interview when you are pulling from the very depths of your brain to use the words that only a highly educated, worldly person would know, and if you stumble or use the wrong phrase, you cringe and feel like the fraud you think you are? Feeling as though surely they see it, of course they do because they are in the position of hiring, at an advantage, so of course they can see right through you. Here's the thing: nobody's perfect, and no one person always says the right thing and uses the exact word needed at that exact moment needed.

Sure, there are many people in the world with expansive and downright impressive vocabularies. Let alone those with IQs to rival Albert Einstein, Isaac Newton, and Thomas Edison, or better yet the young lady who at the tender age of twenty-five was appointed as a judge in South Carolina (go Jasmine Twitty!). For every person like them there was an average citizen of non-particular intelligence who also made their way using language (body, verbal, and written), street smarts, and general savvy to make their mark in the world. I say all this to show what *does* matter. What I have tried for years to explain to my children is that your looks, good or bad, and what is on a piece of a paper—test or résumé—are only part of the equation. What you say, the language you use, and your ability to converse all matter just as much.

Here's the kicker: in many instances your ability to speak carries you far and if you happen to be one of the few who not only mastered your native tongue but those of others, then you could just as well make a way out of no way at all. In today's society, language and the ability to speak with a person no matter their level is indispensable. That in no way means you can't speak Ebonics (also known as AAVE, African American Vernacular English) or use slang liberally, but it does mean that you recognize there is a time and place for all things, and you have the wits about you to distinguish between them.

I am one of those smart dumb people who walks around with hopes and dreams of changing the world. I have amassed quite a bit of street savvy, and if you combine that with my natural curiosity and ability to absorb skills and knowledge of things that interest me, I am very at odds with my lack of that higher education discussed earlier. I enjoy engaging in conversation that will expand my awareness and interest, but that doesn't translate well on paper or even at first glance. So, what does a girl without credentials do to advance beyond the limits society puts on her mentally and professionally?

You work harder, you try to do more, and you say yes to every opportunity you can feasibly manage. You expand your horizon one experience at a time. Fake it till you make it. Sometimes that's all you can do. All the while you work on improving yourself, and that doesn't mean that you must attend a school, but you can always take a class, attend a seminar, or simply pick up a book and struggle your way through it, using

Google like we used to use a dictionary. Force yourself, your mind, and your understanding to expand beyond your limitations of today and try to enjoy the discomfort you feel. Those feelings of being a fraud are actually the feeling of breaking through to your next triumph out of pure effort. You didn't allow your present to hinder your future, and for that you should be proud.

Lesson 8

Speech Tells A Lot About Who You Are

Growing up in Miami, I had the opportunity to learn from many different cultures simply by existing within them. Who doesn't know that Miami is as big a melting pot as New York? We Miamians are proud to live in a city that collects so many different cultures, mostly because that means in one day you can eat Jamaican-, Cuban-, Haitian-, and African-influenced foods, and still go home to enjoy some good ole Southern cooking. Yes, as far as I am concerned Miami is still a part of the South!

If you couldn't speak to people, no matter their background, in a manner that was not only respectful but understandable, then you would quickly find yourself in what *The Boondocks'* character Huey called a "nigger moment." Okay listen, before you even begin to get upset by my use of the word nigger, don't. I despise the word as much as the next person and its use at this moment is simply to draw a comparison to the actions of different people when addressed in a manner unbecoming. Because that's exactly what the word was created to describe something unbecoming, undesirable.

Actually, that in itself is a perfect segue; how many time have I heard people say "my nigger" and then a conversation continues without a pause? Why do we still continue to degrade ourselves by using this phrase? At this point, it's not just within the black communities, youths as a collective toss around the word nigger without regard or disparity. They will ever defend their right to make use of it as a term of friendly companionship and sincerity or endearment only said to a trusted friend. They are blind to the affronting gall of its defense. Come on, how can I not break down the use of saying *"my,"* a possessive adjective describing a sense of ownership and belonging, as well as "nigger," which we all know was intended to be a derogatory term to devalue a race, class, and color of a specific set of people.

Here's the thing, I recognize that the use of the word among us was seen as a part of excelling or moving past that period of time and elevating ourselves, "taking it back," as I've heard people say before. It was an effort to show ourselves capable of standing among those who once stood above us, or at least that's what I understand the intention to be. But why haven't we just eliminated the use of the word entirely?

Okay, I clearly got off track with this specific subject matter so allow me to reign myself back in and get to back to the overall point. For as long as can be remembered language has always separated citizen from a citizen. A person that spoke using the proper tongue was seen as educated, cultured and coming from a family of means without ever having proof of either. This assumption was further advanced by the lack of comparable education opportunities for minorities. A well-spoken person of any nationality other than white was an affront to society.

If you are able to speak of things past your immediate section of life then you must have received some amount of education; if you are worldly and able to speak of current events, then it can be assumed that you not only completed your primary education requirement but that you advanced in school and possibly attended college. If you are able to enunciate complex words and know the proper use of words—such as "to" versus "too," "they're" versus "there," and the favorite of the most scholars, "your" versus "you're"—then you are automatically assumed to be intelligent and knowledgeable. You also get points by being able to have a conversation without saying "cause," "like," "um," or words that don't actually exist in the modern version of Webster's dictionary—if you can't, then you are almost as immediately dismissed as undeserving of anything of quality and substance.

So, what do I tell my children about the importance of language? Nothing actually, the better question is what do I *show* them. Yes, among friends and family you should be relaxed and can speak in a common manner, as people with a Caribbean heritage usually speak (including patois, Creole, Spanglish, etc.) and using words that may not be common when speaking to someone with no Caribbean exposure at all. My children have seen me talk several ways in different situations. I have a tendency to develop an accent seemingly from nowhere when around friends or when speaking to another person who has a pronounced accent, but when out in the general public I without consciousness or intent tend to speak in a more proper manner, for which kids used to tease me and say I sound white.

Truth be told, I hate that summation. To say that when a person uses proper etiquette and verbiage means they "sound white" is to imply that only white (Caucasian specifically) people ever had that ability. I have attempted for years to remind those I come across that how you speak is a precursor to all of life; it can open as well close doors for you long before you've had the chance to polish yourself up and be formally presented. Just a little food for thought.

9

At this point I have discussed topics related to adolescence, but we all know that is hardly the end of growth. Actually it's probably better said that the growing ages of birth to twenty are a mere preface to the true stages of learning that you embark upon. It's what happens when you are not only legal to the eyes of the world but also responsible for your own existence that counts most. No more mommy and/or daddy to make the tough decision for you, no guarantees of a hot meal or a ride to whatever you view as important. No, once you are beyond the responsibility of your parents is when you learn what true growth is.

Up until the point that your actions truly only impact *your* life and direction. After hitting adulthood, the blame can no longer be placed upon those who raised you, so only then do you begin to value all the freedom you had before—and yes, there was freedom in youth. You were free to just exist. You went to sleep, you ate, you bathed, you dressed, you existed simply by opening your eyes each day and closing them each evening. You were not concerned—hell, it probably wasn't even on your radar to be worried about how you existed. What's more is that you thought you were entitled to things. I'm sure you thought that having the best clothes of your choosing and no less was a right, that being groomed and escorted around was what a parent was supposed to do, I mean it's not like they had other things that were more important to do than waiting for you to finish or begin a new sport, new school, or new relationship, right?

Wrong! And your moment of achieving adulthood is when you will begin to see this for yourself. The day a person dares to step out on their own, truly on their own, is the day their heart feels appreciation of all that was done for them before. Because it's not until there is no food in the magic fridge—shoot, maybe no fridge at all—do you recognize there is no magic involved. The magic lay in the hands of the people you saw as parents, not actual people. Your parents experienced the same shock as you are now at some point, and what's more, they had to do it generations before you, before the technical advancements we all share today and there is no denying that technology has been beneficial to all areas of life. The magic is in the work: the tireless efforts to make ends meet, and to find love and stay within that love so that you have a better perspective of the world and its possibilities. There is nothing harder than adulting, it's the idea of what you thought being an adult would be. The funny thing is that perspective is the true beauty of childhood, as a child it was all magical, you couldn't understand the responsibilities that is inherit to being an independent person in the world., but to be an adult is all that you have dreamed of ever since you could remember. You wanted to be one, you wanted to be able to sleep late, drink, and come and go as you please without question. As it says in Corinthians 13:11 (New King James version), "When I was a child, I spoke as a child, I thought as a child, I reasoned like a child..." Now the day has come, and if you are anything like I was, you are not prepared.

Lesson 9

What They Don't Teach You in School: Life Sucks Skills

So the coolest thing once you reach middle school is that you begin to take multiple classes; you no longer have one primary teacher for all the core classes, instead you may have as many as seven. This usually begins around the seventh or eighth grade, usually the first occasion of you being in control of what brings you joy, otherwise known as your electives. If you have parents like mine they will try to control this as well, but still, you get to choose something—maybe the same class as your friend, or a class that would allow you to have the same lunch time as your friends, or boy- or girlfriend It's around this time that I felt my first sense of true autonomy, that my destiny was my own, which didn't take long for my parents to correct. I wanted to take something as frivolous as drama (no drama isn't frivolous but that's what my parent thought), so they made me take home economics instead. I was not happy, and so began my obsession with choice. This is when you desire to choose things rears its ugly little head because you have begun see an end to your life as a child. By the ninth grade your point of view is that you only have four more years and then that's it, your life begins and nobody, especially your parents, gets to tell you what you can or can't do. (I mean you can't legally drink even then, but we all know there are ways around that.) Maybe you'll choose a college, maybe you'll go off and become the next big things in music or movies, maybe you'll just leave and never come back. Possibilities are endless, and they are the sole reason for getting through the next four years as quickly as possible. School to you is a formality, something you just gotta do because "they" say you have to, not because you don't already know everything there is to know about life. Meanwhile, parents and schools are trying to work in tandem to prepare your clueless self for life and all that it will bring.

Well, what I have come to understand is that when it comes to life skills, parents and schools both fail. The goal of education is to teach us the history of things, no matter the subject, be it math, science, reading, history, or any other subject you can think of; they all teach you about what was, what has been, and what is currently happening. Although all that information is helpful and instrumental in understanding the world and your path in it, I admit none of it has anything to do with the future, or more specifically your future.

School and often parents don't teach children tangible life skills, the skills they will need in the future to help them survive—and not just survive, but thrive and live life more abundantly. This is something that really needs to change, and it needs to change sooner rather than later because the world doesn't stop spinning and people don't stop growing, but the quality, abilities, and cognitive functioning skills of adults are slowing. More and more working-class and able-bodied people are less equipped to deal with the many lessons and decision that will be thrust upon them. So why aren't schools including a course on life skills?

Also, why aren't parents aware that although they mean well and have every intention of raising a well-rounded individual, the business of living interferes with all their good intentions? Adults are too busy being adults to realize that they—*we*—are failing to prepare children to do the same. Yes, we know we have to teach them manners, economics, and maybe even how to cook but we don't see the need to teach them how to balance a checkbook, how to write a letter, how to pay bills, and how to invest and save.

We stress the importance of the first impressions, but we ought to teach them how to interact in a business setting, how one should go about advancing oneself, and how to interact with others socially and publicly. We encourage them to see the world, but we fail to show them how. Of course, it's not intentional—parents assume that teachers and coaches are imparting the wisdom of life you as a parent might not remember, and teachers and coaches may assume the same of the parents. But at the end of the day, the business of adulting is hard enough without either party realizing the lack of preparation young people have received when expecting them to become fully functional adults.

So, what is the solution; awareness, community and a reboot of the educational focuses? If we have any hopes of securing all of our futures, we need to invest wholeheartedly in our footprints and those that will walk in them.

As I finished that last line, it occurred to me that how to invest in our children is not as obvious as it used to be. Fifty or so years ago, our fathers and mother put all their efforts, hopes,

and dreams into their children and found ways to take care of
their families, often by working themselves into early graves to
send the children onto to college or to start a business that the
family could be proud of. Why did that value system ever breaks
down? Why did we as a society ever decide that being a parent
wasn't good enough? No, we needed to be the good guy in all
things. We exchanged discipline for dual decision-making, we
chose friendship instead chastisement, we chose to turn a blind
eye to the early bad actions of a child in lieu of standing firm to
the truth that a lack of rules creates wanton and often
disturbing behavior.

Here's the truly sad part: we as adults created a
generation of people who are ill-equipped to handle life and the
struggles it holds. We have created a generation that believes
their own high ideals should be honored and manifested simply
because they did what they were supposed to do. If you look
around you, we have the entitled college students who don't
believe in working their way up a ladder; instead they truly feel
that as they receive their diplomas, degrees, and certificates
that doors will open up to them complete with all the knowledge
ever needed. They don't see the value in the struggle, and they
don't know how to appreciate the hard work that went into
getting there. But can we blame them?

Maybe you don't even see why these scenarios are an
issue. Is it really a crime to want to give them an easier life?
Wasn't that the entire point of your ancestors working as hard
as they did, so the next generation wouldn't have to? Of course,
there is truth and merit in that argument—but ask yourself
this: if we fail to test the line to ensure it can hold the weight
that is bound to be placed upon its shoulders, then who should
be blamed when the very structure come crumbling down and

we are thrust into a more archaic existence than ever before? Do we blame those who knew better, or do we turn our backs once again and say nothing, closing the curtain around the mess instead of examining how we all played a role in its demise? *We* have to build the strong foundation.

10

What is your routine when you open your eyes each day? Do you open your eyes and mentally check off your things to do, do you reconcile all the intended task from the day or week before that didn't get completed? Or, do you start every day daydreaming about all the things you would like to do, not the stuff you know you must do but like hey I would really like to go out tonight, or catch up with your bestie and grabs a few drinks. How do you begin your day? Or do you drag yourself out of bed, maybe turn on the news and passively listening for traffic or bad weather that would derail you from taking an extra five minutes to laze about your room or closet? Get dressed, wake kids, parents, pets, and etc., make coffee, tea, or toast? Thusly, breaking in another day. All of these autonomic steps are how you begin and often end each day but how many of people begin the new day with thanks in their heart, mind, and soul.

No, I am not speaking from a religious standpoint. I am talking about how the task of beginning your day rarely leaves most people time to be grateful for having a life to begin. Regardless of what you believe in or don't believe in, every day brings about something to be grateful for. Be it that you were able to open your eyes, or that at least one of the two hundred things you set forth to do actually gets done, there is something to be thankful for.

Why should just living make you happy? Well, let's think about it. How much would it suck if yesterday was your last day of actively breathing? What if yesterday's complaints, arguments, and lack of acknowledgment of how blessed you are to walk, talk, and think independently ceased to happen. What if your last impression upon the world was about something meaningless, something that was completely within your control to change? What if you never again get to sleep late on a rainy weekend, or catch up with a really good friend over a meal? You know what I mean, one of those restorative conversations you can only have with a person who has known your good times and stood beside you through the bad. I have some pretty great girlfriends, and that alone would make me want to cry, never being able to see them again. But there is so much more! What if yesterday you didn't remember to tell your children, your lover, your mother, or your father that you loved them? Worse still if your last conversation with them was a critique. Now you wake up this morning, and you are unable to speak, or hear, stand, or breathe.

Does this thought make you value your next day a little more?

Would you wake up a little more grateful if the life you woke up to actually reflecting your innermost desires and dreams? I'm not just talking about money. What if anything were obtainable? Would that make that first breathe a little more valuable?

I hope so...

Lesson 10

Bad Times Don't Last for Long, But the Type of Life You Choose to Lead Can Be Unending in Its Misery

God said the meek shall inherit the earth.

What God *didn't* say was we should live life in the shadows, yet many of us, including myself, do. We draw into the energy of others without ever igniting our own fires. Actually, let's be precise here; it has taken me three and a half years to get to this line in this my third book. Yes, my third. As I may have mentioned before, I generally love writing, and it is very much my passion and my release. However, I have never had faith in myself, and therefore I never considered this could be my livelihood. I prompted, promoted, embraced, and absorbed the energy of others without ever—and I do mean ever— thinking that I may only have *today* to make my mark. But it's true, I only have today to show the world that there is more to me than my smile.

I've been married for ten years, and in that time, I have spent all of my energy encouraging my children and my husband to not allow the world to shrink their greatness. Especially my children; I have invested in their minds, exposing them to different cultures and perspectives and having conversations with them about the world as it is, not as I would like it to be. My husband, who happens to be a bit world-trodden (he's been beaten up by life), I constantly encourage him that it's never too late to start again or start over and not be afraid to fail. Failure doesn't mean that you are not good enough, or that an idea doesn't have merit, failure is just another step in your ladder to success. I would not allow his failure to be a reflection of our efforts and I wanted our children to know it's never too late to try. I stand by all this but truth is I never ever practiced what I preached. Of course, in my mind, I was doing what I am supposed to do...and then my perspective was knocked on its ass.

What stops us from being everything that we are and more is us. We hear people (celebrities, authors, musicians, poets, scientist, academics, actors, etc.) say to never let anyone stop you from achieving your goals. Although they have a point and are correct in their intent, let's examine the real-world view. What we need is a belief in ourselves and to acknowledge the reason(s) why we may not. I knew from an early age that I wanted more, and that despite my environment I would have to find a way to get the more that I craved. But I never knew what the more was, or even how to achieve it, and of course I made many, *many* mistakes along the way. However, I knew I wouldn't settle for what I saw. I refused the idea that all I could have was a job and maybe a decent apartment close to where I grew up. I certainly refused to accept that I would never see any parts of the world other than the neighboring counties or states. This thinking was revolutionary among my neighbors; many of them were just happy to rent a house. If you were lucky enough to own it, well damn, then you had made it. You were living life. Meanwhile you may have to accept that sexual abuse and promiscuity were all part of the package of growing up; it was almost like a weeding out process, all worth it if in the end you land a guy (in many cases a mid-range drug dealer) and he takes care of all your bills. This was the norm when growing up in lower-class, often black neighborhoods, this was all to be expected and never discussed, it's just the way life goes.

How dare I want more! Did I know what was out in the world? ... well, neither did anyone around me, but whatever it was perceived to be scarier than staying put. The caveat was in accepting that the life I saw was a good one. It wasn't until I made new friendships and they told me their stories, their adventures, their goals only then did I realize there was so much more to hope for.

What I figured out was that as long as I was exposed to more, I wanted more. So, wouldn't the reverse work as well?

Lesson 10 is just that simple. Seize the day is good and all, but imagine what a world filled with individuals who have both exposure and desire in their everyday environment would look and feel like. I believe it would make for a world worth inheriting.

No one wants to inherit trash.

11

In today's environment, it is so easy to get wrapped up in the bad. We have so many negative stories, both in the news and what is shared in and around social media. In the last ten years, I've heard more about earthquakes, hurricanes, tornadoes, and other deadly storms wiping out upward of two hundred people at a time, each storm. All of which are reminders that Mother Nature can and always has had the power to bring us all to our knees. We dismiss these occurrences as nothing more than timing and bad luck, and we go about our way, happily oblivious lives until the next thing comes around. We organize relief drives, fundraisers, and other activities and we say we stand together—but then what? Then there are the man-made traumas of the world, the shooting, stabbing, bombing, and more of men, women, and children who lose their lives due to the obscurity of justice and righteousness of a few. If you combine these to factors, don't you feel how truly small you are?

When life is not promised, should a person, a family, or a country value its occupants more than we do?

One of my more preferred life reminders is, "The definition of insanity is doing the same thing over and over again and expecting a different result." Well, it combines well with the adage about history repeating itself. These are sayings many of us know and use, yet round and round the hamster wheel we continue to go. We perpetuate the same atrocities every day, every year, and every decade or so, and it appears we haven't learned a damn thing.

Let me say it for you—who the hell am I to stand in judgment of another? (I hear you saying this with righteous indignation so please don't disappoint me.) I am no one special— but that's the beauty of me being the writer of this book, I get to say what I want and if you want to argue with me…well, write your own book. Currently, it is popular to identify yourself as being a feminist or to agree with and be vocal about the Black Lives Matter movement. Yet women and black folks (African American if you want to be polite) are still the most impeded groups of the world. Women berate and belittle each other, and many align themselves with men who further the notion of a "woman's place" despite acknowledging their heavy dependence on them. Men love to sexualize and/or maternalize women as they see fit but they can't seem to separate themselves from between their hips, lips, and thighs. How's that for an enigma. To that effect black lives only seem to matter when impeded upon by white lives; we seem to do a great job of shortening the lifespan of each other without any assistance or cause.

Let's be honest: *man* is a greater destroyer of things than Mother Nature could ever be! Now let me take the fun out of your criticism; I am absolutely stating a very unpopular opinion and on any given day of the week I will be willing to argue the exact opposite of what I just said, but that is just because I like to debate things as a way to expand a person's way of thinking and evaluating a point of view, and you are welcome to do the same. What I want to make clear is that saying man is a great destroyer isn't a condemnation of man or a call to beware of the climate. My goal is to say that if your life is so subject to outside influences of people, places, and things, then shouldn't you care more about what you do, how you do it, and what or how much you are exposed to?

Lesson 11

You Are What You Eat, In Thought, Word, And Deed, But You Can't Diet Away Your Pain

Now, much like the initial surge of the Harlem Renaissance, is a great time to be alive.

As a Bahamian American black woman, I embrace the multicultural presence in America, and being from Miami I can't help but embrace every nationality. Actually, saying that I embrace them is pretentious as hell in my eyes because no one person requires my acceptance of their being for them to exist and thrive. Yet as an American, if I bought into the entitlement of those fairer-skinned than myself, then I would believe that it is my born right to permit someone else's existence. I would also have to buy into the ridiculous notion that being a woman means that I require a man to teach, tell, and show me the way.

Just in case you didn't read but chose to skim the content of this book, allow me to summarize the first two chapters clearly and refute that notion all at once. My momma didn't play that game, and neither do I.

I was raised by wonderfully *strong*, independent women who were or are revered by the men they *chose* to spend their lives with. No one person has the right to dictate how another has to live, just as no one person should corral, correct, or steer the paths of another. I am not sure when this point of view became the main hold of a particular group, I am not even sure that I could ever understand the loathing they have for people of a varying chromatic makeup than themselves, but I am certain that no one was born to be judge, juror, and executioner of all people. Yet still, we who suffer under those presumptions give up that power freely and without protest because of an ingrained fear within all of us.

We all share a fear of the unknown and being unknown. Everyone wants to matter to someone because everyone's shared fallacy is the desire to be adored, whether it be in a loving healthy way or for what we possess. Whether we seek love familially, or love, admiration, and envy for what we have or how we look, desire is in all of us. These desires have led to the devaluation of depth and modesty. Greed and cruelty are deep flaws of today's society and have been accepted as the norm. We don't know how to work together, and we don't know how to share the spotlight and diversify our outlook among us.

We imbibe poisonous and toxic behavior, and only when truly wounded do we cry out for help from those we seek to destroy, and then in the most traitorous ways we vilify those few who have worked at bringing us together and are refusing to accept less any longer. Bless those who say you can and should want more, you can and will do better, you can be stronger, and I will do my part to assist you in getting there. But then others respond, *no*, we can't accept that. No, we won't stand for being uncomfortable and ashamed. No, we won't embrace change because for years we have gotten by on our excuses and fears. You can't really expect us to stand up and fight for our own piece of the proverbial pie.

However, I do see the light, a beacon beginning to shine through the BS of all bad behavior. There are times that we come together as a collective... Not as a black man or woman agreeing with a white man or woman, or as Americans assisting another nation, but as a group that can not only agree but emphasizes as a whole than no person deserves to be preyed upon, discriminated against, or devalued. We are humans who are beginning to understand we all have something to lose if this type of behavior is allowed to continue. We share in the desire to have rights and privileges according to our beliefs.

I want the right to bear arms just as much as I want the right to control my body and what I do with it. I am neither Democrat nor Republican—I am a person who chooses to think independently of that binary. I, as a citizen who is responsible enough to pay my bills and taxes, believe that I should have the right to choose my sexual partners and the expression of my sexuality. The way I lean Democrat is that I choose to help minorities achieve a fairer wage, job opportunities, and education, while I lean Republican when I choose to put my money back into infrastructure, resources, and the continuation of a stable government that has my interest in mind. As a person, I believe that we can only choose one party or another when we have all been counted, observed, accepted, respected, and acknowledged as people who are all part of a whole. We are the monopoly; *we* are the most important resource we have.

So it's past time we act like it.

The summary of people is as complex as a sentence; no matter how simple it may seem it requires structure to be complete.

These last two lessons come without chapters because I have no desire to lighten the seriousness of the lesson. So far, I have tried bring lighthearted awareness to the commonalities of growing up. Yes, my focus was on women because I am one, but also because I am a daughter and a mother. I am in love with women and their replications of God's divine power. He gifted us with the power of pain and endurance—and please believe those are a gift. Without our ability to embrace, handle, and turn pain around, we would not have survived these 300,000 years on this planet. Adam may have been the beginning, but he was not complete until Eve stood by his side, blameless under the scrutiny of God.

Women don't just make lemonade out of lemons, we make pies and cakes! We learn how to capture the essence of what love feels like, what life and breath feel like and use it to brighten up a home. Woman are amazing and I don't give two cents for anyone's contradictory opinion of what I said. If a man can't procreate, he can't judge the power between my limbs.

All that said, welcome to the end. Please understand I wrote this book from a place of love and admiration. It took a lot out of me to get to this point because in the midst of starting this project I lost my first inspiration of all things, my mom. So it was very hard to want to see this through. Still, I knew what I needed to do to finally deal with that void.

Initially I wanted to write this as an abstract daughterly point of view of her parenting skills. In some ways, I kept with that plan, but I didn't know how to deal with her not being around. I don't mind in the physical sense, but I didn't know how to deal with the loss of her presence, her will, and her strength pushing me along. So, when I finally decided to pick up where I left off, it was much harder than I ever thought a single thing could be. My mom may have been difficult to understand and hard to reach, but her love was so much stronger than any person on this planet ever deserved, including her children. Her beauty was outstanding because you could see her strife in every line around her smile, which she didn't give often. Her eyes yelled out at you her physical and emotional pain. Her body wasn't strong enough to contain the ferocity of her affection, and her lack of hesitancy to protect those she loved most, her children and grandchildren.

So, in honor of the woman who sparked the greatest love I will ever know, this is how I have chosen to leave you: without apology. The last two lessons are about what we need to do if we are to have a future worth looking forward to.

Lesson 12

Evolution is Necessary

What goes around, comes around, right? The first law of thermodynamics states, "Energy can neither be created nor destroyed." Don't worry, I didn't decide all of a sudden to become a master of hyperbole. I am simply using age-old wisdom to make my point in a broad way. Humans are in the midst of a bad cycle of self-deprecation and self-mutilation, and for the life of me I can't understand how we got here, but history tells me we've been here before. We have created an atompsehere in which people thrive by tearing down others in an effort to bring attention to ourselves and our beliefs, even if we haven't formed our own platform yet. America claims to be bigger and better than it has been in the past, having more access to health, wealth, and power than other countries could dream of, but we are losing on all worldly fronts. Our education system is broken because we don't empower teachers to teach—our children have the shakiest value system I've ever seen. They believe technology trumps all things and that they are owed a modicum of respect without ever extending respect themselves. Many of them believe the world is indebted to them because they are able to decipher it faster and with less of a footprint than before. Yet they know nothing about actual survival.

Perhaps this problem started in the late '70s and early '80s, when the goal was to develop faster, bigger, brighter, and bolder technology. We are the true birthers of technology, right, we are the ones who strove to take computers from the mega mainframes that were first introduced while we were in grade school to the ever-accessible laptop, iPad, and smartphones we can't even get a toddler to put down. That is, if a laptop isn't too cumbersome for today's youth! This is what we worked for: new and improved ways to connect people around the world and new ways to improves resources, knowledge, and access to the world at large. It was meant to improve our lives, but did it? I mean, a person could of course make an argument that it did—now you can be bullied all over the globe, not just in your neighborhood! Now folks can sit in their most comfortable chair and tell you what's wrong with your...hell, everything, meanwhile never getting off their ass to do something as simple as comb their hair.

Oh and let me not ignore the power of exclusion and rejection in today's society. Women have been especially affected by this, as we have always been told to conform to a man's standard of beauty and acceptable behavior. We used to use these atrocities as a binding agent, bringing us together and finding common ground, working to bring each other up. Early on admittedly it was within the race and social standings we related to, but nonethless the feeling of being oppressed by men who could only do a fourth of what a woman was responsible for increased the compassion we had for one another. These days, well, not so much, and it makes me feel really sad. Women are more defined by the ideals of men and a harsh society than never before. Women are actually killing themselves by augmenting their bodies and minds in order to be percieved as more desirable. Women are injecting all types of unknown and known chemicals into their butts, faces, and lips to replicate a seemingly preferred "type" of women. Individuality is only acceptable if you are exceptionally beautiful. Meanwhile the makeup industry is in its most profitable era ever. We spend millions if not billions of dollars making ourselves look further removed from who we are than ever before. Makeup used to be used to enhance your natural beauty—now it is used to hide and transform a person into what equates to someone else's ideal view of what a woman should be. All of this is in the name of evolution, right? I mean, we are growing and this is what the future says we need to be. Or is it?

I believe we couldn't be futher away from loving ourselves and growing. We are broken right down to the core and I'm not sure we even know it.

So what happens next? What is the next step in human evolution? What will tomorrow's woman look like? Will she still be able to creat life if her waist line has been permently cinched through years if dieting, restricitive clothing, and surgery? Will she be able to provide for herself outside of the bedroom and social entertainment? Will tomorrow's woman know her true power comes from a place other than the apex of her legs and thighs? Will she be able to raise children strong enough to be productive citizens in a world that is filled with enough toxins and waste that it could destroy all our natural food sources? Hell, I don't know, but I know that today's woman makes for some very entertaining TV.

Lesson 13
(Purposely and perfectly odd)

"I Hope That You're the One—If Not, You Are the Prototype" – Andre 3000

My last lesson is all about the inspiration for this book: the women in my life. Now to clarify, when I say the women in my life, it doesn't mean that I know them all. I have been influenced negatively and positively by women near and far and being a stranger doesn't lessen their ability to have influenced me personally. It simply means that women are the biggest influence in my personal life. It's the plights, pain, triumphs, hurdles, and achievements of women both near and far, and living and dead, that have influenced my life the most. Of course, this could be because I am a woman and as a member of this superior species I readily identify with my shared sex. It could be said that I identify with the strength and resilience of women through the years.

Woman are the backbones of all societies.

See how I let that stand there all by itself? That's because I intended it to be declarative. Women are everything that is right and wrong in this world. Women are magnificent and otherworldly, and men know it. Women, this last chapter is dedicated to you, just as the first was an opening about women who influenced me, the last shall be my lasting impression of your strength and magnitude. A woman being of man was the first display of our being created from love and intended to sustain and strengthen our counter-sex. When we stand together, we move mountains and part seas—as noted in the response to our most recent election. There is a womanhood movement currently rocking our country just as it was during the years of the woman's suffrage movement. The change is swift and can be felt immediately when we come together. Our affirmation is that we will no longer *allow* ourselves to be treated as lesser citizens, and that we will no longer *allow* ourselves to be harrassed or cajoled into accepting "our place" in life. When we stopped suffering in silence, thinking and feeling alone and defeated before we even tried anything, we then allowed ourselves to dream bigger and bolder things. We have always held vast potential and we have only known pain and strife, so why can't we create the change we desperately need to see in the world? There is a reckoning coming that the world has not felt in about a century and all I can think is, Why did it takes us this long?

This is not a denial of the power and virility of men; it is an observance of how much our submission to them has both granted and denied us to be as wonderful as we are.

Women have given men the power to believe.

One of my most believed sheroes is Maya Angelou. Here is a woman admired by the world for just being herself, and for her own understanding that she mattered, that she deserved to be loved, to be seen, and to be heard. Her grandeur emanated from her before she ever opened her mouth, yet she did not speak for years because at an early age she understood her power and properly feared what it could do if unchecked. When I heard her speak my soul listened and understood that I am a blessed because I am woman in the world today.

Over my short forty years of life, I have come in contact with many amazing examples of womanhood. Women of varying ethnicities, various backgrounds, and social standings, women old and young with saddening similarities of building themselves back up after trauma, abuse, neglect, and/or ignorance, and still they stand tall and counsel, console, and help bolster the men in their lives, gently guiding their paths forward. They become heads of state or heads of industry, and still allow their husbands to be head of the household. What feats indeed.

Behold the lady.

I must admit though that today's woman happens to be my favorite version. She is unapologetically her; she stands taller in her shame than she ever could pretending to be ashamed for wanting the same as a man. She is proud of the mystique of her sex and is earnest about her desire to have more and be seen as more. She seeks recognition for her ability to handle all the pressures of a man and still raise a family. Today's women are proud of their many hues, and will not allow society to dictate what is viewed as beautiful. Beauty comes in every shade, every height, and every size. While she does not condone the tragedies of her past, the woman of today refuses to allow her past to dictate her future.

Today's woman does not wait to be invited into the room—she will build her own walls, never closing the door behind her but offering open arms to any others who care to come along. Today's woman is a lioness, fierce, proudly forging her own way.

The me I see when I look in the mirror is not quite there yet, but I am open to being broken down so that my rebuilt self will be unbreakable. I used to apologize for not being cute enough, smart enough, or sexy enough, for not being sorry about my sexuality and sexual desires. I apologized for being smart without a degree. Most of all, I apologized for wanting things that my present circumstances couldn't produce. That was the first thing to go. Why should a person apologize for wanting more?

These women whom I say have influenced me worked too damn hard to allow me to settle for less than my worth. They have shown me we are resilient enough to create whole companies just to make a better world for our chidren to grow up in. They have reinvented themselves over and over, and have set standards that people will follow for decades still yet to come. The modern day woman knows the power of a smile. She knows when she places her hands on her hips others shrink away. She also knows the strength of the love she has to give; should she decide to adorn you in her affection, you will feel seven feet tall and unstoppable. These modern women, all women, are magnificent in their complexities. Women reading, if you take no other lesson from this collection of words I was arrogant enough to record, please take this: Do not surrender to the ideals of another. You are beautiful and all that is needed for the world to go on. You deserve to be admired for your ability to fight for all that you love. Your decisiveness and independence are only matched by your ability to reach out and accept that we are all fallible.

Women are the personification of every religion because *grace* lies within our very being.

Acknowledgments

Thank you for supporting, indulging in, dare I say even reading this collection of thoughts. It has truly been a journey, and even as I write these last sentences, I feel a sense of completeness and joy I have rarely experienced in my life. This is my love letter to every woman I have ever known, and I do mean all of them. I am smart enough to know that whether she was friend or foe, every woman I encountered has helped to create the woman that was able to put this all together. This collection of words has come from the knowledge that is gained from living life. God's gift to me was my ability to quietly observe, remember and record.

My introspection fuels my admiration and although I say thanks to all I, of course, have my select few I must single out.

To my mother: Your world was full of bitterness and pain, and yet you found the capacity to love and transfer all that love to me and mine. You are no longer here for your flowers and hugs, but I know you knew that I admired you every day and in every way and admiration I have for you still. I love you to the heavens and back.

To my aunts and grandmother: You all taught me first, and I am ever so grateful. My grandmother's name was probably my first precursor to our strength, Pearl. Special thanks to my Aunt G, you've never looked at me without love in your heart and eyes, you answer my every call, and you always remind me that I am amazing even when I'm not. You hold all my pieces when I fall apart, and when I go too far of course you create a beacon that brings me back home. I love you so much more than you know. Thank you for catching me every time.

To my sweet circle of friends: There are six of you whom I depend on to correct, direct, and refocus me when I've gone too far left, and I couldn't love you more. I have never worked to change a single a thing about you, yet we all find ways to help each other grow. You are my family, my friends, and more than sisters could ever be because of your love for me is voluntary. I will *always* be there for each of you. Thank you.

To the women of CI: You could never know just how much I admire your paths, strength, and will. You ladies really showed me what being a grown-ass woman looks like. You had the strength to live one life and still come back to breathe life for someone who you saw as deserving. Thank you for showing me how it's done.

To the women I call my own: Wow! A mother could never be as proud as I am of you three. I am proud of your openness, I am proud of your talents, I am proud of the compassion and consideration. I am *proud* of you!

Last but never least, to my mother-in-law (love): You created my best friend and love, you accepted me when the waters were mostly cloudy, you loved me without an exception or asterisk, and you call us all your own. Words cannot express the depth of gratitude I have for you. Now let's make some kickskirts!

Thank you all.

About the Author

Well what can I say? I could tell you that this book was a passion project and not my normal genre of interest. I'd like to say that I am a developing communitist (an activist for a sense of community) if only that were a word. I am a mother first and foremost and have been since I decided to have my first child at the tender age of nineteen. I am a wife, a sister, a daughter, and hopefully a very good friend to all those around me.

I believe in the power of goodness and grace, but I am an even greater fan of live and let live. I believe in the power of community and family.

I sacrificed most of my wants and dreams throughout my adult life to raise my children to the best of my abilities and it is only now at the blessed age of forty-plus that I am allowing myself to dream and dream big. I began this book sometime in 2015 and it started off as a way to get my mother to open up, to talk about the only thing I knew brought unabashed joy. The more we discussed the similarities between her raising me and my brothers and me raising her grandchildren, the more the idea of sharing this knowledge gained power. . After my mother passed away in 2016, it was hard to want to start writing again. Once I restarted, finishing this was the only thing on my mind.

So here you have it. This is a project created from a place of love and adoration for all we women go thru, will ever go thru and are still going through in our lifetime.

Hopefully, my daughters won't think I embarrased them and should have kept my thoughts to myself. I actually only care a little about that. This is for them, this is for all my sister friends, my aunts, my grandmother, my nieces, this is what my love looks like in words.